9/11: Critical Incident

9/11: Critical Incident

Dr. Ron Mercer, PhD, LMHC

A true account of critical incident counseling delivered (CISD)
to the victims of September 11, 2001, in the lower Manhattan
and surrounding New York area.

Print information available on the last page.

Rev. date: 07/26/2019

To order additional copies of this book, contact:
Xlibris
1-888-795-4274
www.Xlibris.com
Orders@Xlibris.com
561895

My thanks goes out to Andrea Zoller of Knock-out Graphics for the excellent job she did on my cover.

Preface

The following narrative, or memoir if you prefer, is a first-person account of the work of a critical incident psychotherapist. These clinicians are typically called into very extreme situations, i.e., natural disasters, catastrophic accidents, to counsel and help ease the emotional pain of the victims of such events. Dr. Ron Mercer, a clinical critical incident therapist from South Florida, had recently completed a report on his work with a hotel staff member who aguishly had witnessed a man commit suicide. The guest at the hotel was an elderly gentleman, who because of his life events having pushed him beyond the threshold of his tolerance, had decided to bring an abrupt end to his earthly suffering and jumped ten stories to his final destination; the atrium floor below, committing a horrific and gruesome suicide in West Palm Beach, Florida. Watching this man jump to his death to the lobby floor, like a tiny meteor suddenly impacting and making a crater in the wake of its force, had put this staff member in particular, into severe early Post Traumatic Stress Disorder (PTSD) an emotional, physical, psychological reaction to experiencing an extraordinary, sudden loss of control due to a natural or accidental/man imposed catastrophe or event.

This staff member, a Latino female originally from Ecuador, had similarly witnessed another man jump to his death from a building in Quito, Ecuador, when she was only ten years old. This recent "jumper" was a negative flashback to her unconscious past, a memory piece, she had put locked away in her temporal lobe, hoping never to retrieve, until this man in West Palm Beach decided there was nothing to live for.

Dr. Mercer took some extra time with Alena that afternoon, nursing her through the emotional pain, both past and present. Little did he know, but in a few short days he would be exposed to listening to the incredulous, almost fictionlike, from a "disaster movie," horrific accounts from many people who watched as they ran from the still burning Twin Towers in lower Manhattan on September 11. "The jumpers." Too many innocent people, sons, daughters, fathers, mothers, lovers, janitors, secretaries, executives, all making the same decision—not a suicidal one out of emotional hopelessness and depression, but one of a very different type, jump to their death. A decision that only God could have some reason or plan for. One that no one should ever be confronted with making, like a Jewish mother during the Holocaust being forced by her Nazi captors to choose either son or daughter—only one could live. No one should ever have that decision even appear in their nightmares, no less their reality. The soon-to-be infamous "jumpers" from the Twin Towers on that early morning in September, had to make a similar decision—a certain life ending one—perish in the flames and smoke from the burning wreckage of the two jets that crashed and changed the world forever, or make what was more certainly a proactive, take charge, "control my destiny on some primitive plane," and jump from one hundred stories to the ground below. Dr. Mercer did not know as he counseled Alena, but her reaction to her "jumper" nightmare was a prelude to his work in lower New York City and the surrounding area in the days to come.

Dr. Mercer was just finishing up compiling his notes for this event (the hotel suicide), when he received the call that he was being called upon to fly to New York City, to administer critical incident therapy to individuals who had survived the September 11, 2001, attack on the World Trade Center. Though in private practice, he works as a CISD therapist for several organizational/EAP companies which hire individuals with his training to go to events like the 9/11 tragedy. He informed his clinical support staff at his private practice, for which he is the Co-Director of the Center for Creative Living that he would be going without hesitation. This is his account of the days he spent in the New York and surrounding area six days after the 9/11 tragedy. These are the days which would not only test his professional acumen as a therapist, like they have never been tested before, but which, possibly as was the case for the elderly "jumper," take him to a world where safety and privilege gave in to horror and randomness. A world where thousands of individuals, at one evil, short microcosm of time, would also be pushed past their personal threshold, plummeting, falling into a dark, netherworld. This is his account of 9/11.

Chapter I

Day 1

September 16, 2001

My flight is speeding down the runway. It lifts off the ground. My thoughts soar as I began my journey to the stricken giant of cities in the northeast, Manhattan. I am a trauma specialist. A psychologist trained to help people who have endured horrible, extraordinary experiences. I assist the violated in regaining their personal freedom. I help the grief stricken ease their pain associated with a loss. I help those who survive a catastrophe; only to see another perish, or have to cope with guilt as a survivor. However, I suspect, with all my training and education, nothing has prepared me for what I am about to confront in the city on the Hudson.

This is "my story," a real life, first-person blow-by-blow, cathartic account of my experiences and reflections on those experiences as they are unfolding. I am hoping that the insights, which I share as I counsel direct and indirect victims of the World Trade Center attack that took place on September 11, 2001, just five days earlier, will help both professionals and lay-people alike, when other unforeseen tragedies, which unfortunately are common to history, take place. The aftermath, just five days later. Still smoldering, still the grey ash, still the very distinct smell of death and still the hope for survival and personal victory.

My jet, a sleek Delta cylinder, floats on top of a beautiful, sun illuminated cloud layer. I remember reading that a witness to the attack on September 11, 2001, said that it was a cloudless, clear blue sky over Manhattan when the first jet, with children, grandparents, loved ones from various backgrounds, innocent to the evil intentions of a handful of passengers with a hatred so strong, slammed into Tower 1 of the World Trade Center that fateful morning. A young man recounted, as the billowing smoke poured from the area of the building that had sustained the brunt of the impact, the second "flying bomb," again with innocent brothers and sisters on board, collided into Tower 2 disappearing "like a phantom from a Twilight Zone episode," into its metal and concrete interior. Shortly thereafter, one tower, literally melting from the searing heat created by the explosion of jet fuel, collapsed like a giant pile of pick up sticks, setting debris and a subsequent billowing cloud of gray ash down into the streets of lower Manhattan. The once blue sky was no more. A dark cloud of unspeakable horror and devastation had replaced it.

I looked out the window of my jet, having just gone through some mild turbulence, wondering what was remaining as the cloud of ash and smoke continued to lift, allowing one to see the war zone that was once two proud, erect soldiers symbolizing the wealth and power of American society.

In my mental preparation for my trauma counseling in New York, I tried to tap into personal experiences, as both a child and an adult, where I felt violated, trespassed against, judged or humiliated, but nothing seemed to have any qualitative or quantitative relevance to the probable psychophysical reactions of the victims who I would be treating. I certainly reflected on my own vulnerable moments when someone or something got the best of me, and I felt disempowered, angry, weak and/or frightened. However, I suspected I will soon have a completely new perspective, possibly even rewriting the definition of these human constructs. In the Kabala, Judaic mystical teachings, it is stated that it is not necessary to live in an acute state of chaos and confusion; rather one can connect with the ongoing process of creation. I only hope the individuals who I will be counseling will be able to see or begin to see, beyond the sudden horror that befell them on September 11.

Upon landing at JFK airport with the passengers applauding safe arrival, I continue to observe the lack of security both on the plane and at the airport. I actually walked onto my plane in Fort Lauderdale, Florida with a large carry-on suitcase that was not hand searched at any point. Denial is a strong word.

The ride in the limousine to my pickup juncture in West Chester County proved to be very pleasurable. I shared the trip with two lovely women, mother and daughter, from Hartford, Connecticut, who were just returning from a woman's bonding vacation in Austria. Susan, the daughter, a very bright and attractive woman, probably in her mid twenties discussed how fascinating it was to be with a group of older women in their fifties and sixties. At that point, I sat up, straightened my posture, and sucked in my "gut" (I am a youthful fifty-two) and listened to see how they reflected on individual life experiences. Her mom, who ran the family business, an ice cream shop, had just sold one of the stores in Connecticut. She was simply delightful, talking about the numerous photos of customers she had collected over the years. Her remaining shop was in Woodberry. I would like to go there one day. I think I would have her homemade rum raison ice cream.

I complimented both of them on maintaining, what was an obvious, excellent mother-daughter bond. I thought to myself, as a men's issue and trauma-anger specialist, if more fathers, sons, and men across the globe went on yearly bonding retreats, hiking in the mountains and sharing their life stories around the campfire at night, the world would be a much safer and peaceful place. The aggressors commandeering the planes of 9/11 were all men, Middle-Eastern men, with years, centuries of anger, rage and unresolved hatred. Funny, I just had a strange image. I imagined Osama Bin Laden, the possible financier of 9/11, sitting with a group of Islamic disciples. Instead of encouraging aggression, he used his power to breach the void between his world and ours. Unfortunately, when one looks at aggression and war, thousands of years of history shows the same theme, time and time again—male lust for power, greed and control, and possibly even of a more psychological and intrapsychic level, unresolved oedipal conflict which is manifested on a universal level throughout the ages, men battling men (fathers) the unconscious drive/fear of both the lust of the female object and simultaneous fear of being vulnerable and losing total control to what She stands for.* The limo reached my destination as I bade them farewell. My last thoughts about mom and daughter, a great metaphor for who they were as people, was that in their two weeks in Austria, they spent a total of $50 shopping. They obviously discovered something much more precious, priceless, and intangible during their journey.

My best friend from high school is Hank Varsillo. He was born nearly totally deaf in both ears. Hank and I have been friends since fourth grade. Hank is both a winner and a survivor, and was a little nut as a kid. My first reflection of him was this weird guy, feet raised, and speeding down the steep incline of prosper Avenue on a tricycle, for which he had outgrown five years earlier.

* This last interpretation is a microcosmic clinical perspective on male violent behavior. The author will not go into this component in the writing of this specific book, but in his new book on men's issues, Dr. Mercer elaborates on this kinetic principal of behavior in a much more detailed manner.

Hank and I are like brothers. From two different worlds in some respects but aligned nevertheless. His father, a hard working, angry man owned a gas station. My father was a well-known big band singer and Chamber of Commerce executive. Hank's father thought I was spoiled. He was right, though we were far from wealthy. I was genuinely petrified of Hank's father. I could only imagine the fear that Hank felt. Hank did not deserve his father's displaced aggressions, nor did the victims of 9/11. I will say however, in retrospect, as I think back on Hank's dad, he was man and victim of his own times and upbringing. There was a soft side to Hank's father which we seldom saw but when it did come out, the experience, though I was quite young, gave me hope that even mean and angry men could be kind and giving. Hank's father was a genuinely good and giving person. It was just that he was a victim of his generation. He more than likely felt that if he showed emotion, and his nurturing side, that this would equate to both he and his son not being respected and them both being taken advantage of in the world in general. His style of parenting and discipline were sometimes very harsh and cruel, but I will say one thing, as far as how Hank turned out. Probably because of his fierce conditioning, not letting Hank get away with anything just because he was handicapped (deaf), those extreme measures probably did toughen Hank up. My best friend from childhood had become a successful man in adult American society. Therefore, on those rare moments when I did see Hank's father being kind to both he and I, I remember the surprised and warm feeling that I had and the hope that he would continue in this warm side of his personality more often than not. Not until the writing of this chapter of "9/11" had I realized the impact that Hank's father had on my early developing thoughts and views on men, their motivations, drives and fears, oftentimes enshrouded by the veil of anger and rage.

It is interesting, as I am dictating this portion of my memoirs of 9/11 and my interpretation of those events, I am sitting in my clinical office and though we have soundproofing in our walls you can sometimes hear a therapy session going on in the room next to mine. That is happening at this moment and I must say that it strikes of the concept of Jung, of synchronicity, how things, time, and events cross or even collide together at random intervals seemingly fitting so well together as a perfect match in a jigsaw puzzle. One of the clinicians in our office, very soft as well as savvy in her own way, is conducting a session with an elderly male patient. Hearing his voice through the walls, I can definitely detect he is from the New York City area possibly Queens, Brooklyn, Staten Island. Ironically, he is speaking of his younger years growing up and working in the city and the need to work hard and try hard to be the best man he could be, oftentimes without the recognition he needed or wanted. This is ironic because the same gentleman was talking several weeks ago with his wife in a session (I have to talk with this clinician to lower the volume, as this is quite difficult and discordant with therapeutic privacy to hear) they were discussing their perceptions of each other and their life. She was very condescending and judgmental, though I am sure there is more to their story than I am presenting, I just remember his reaction sounding very humiliated, not appreciated. I find this element of synchronicity, as I always do, quite interesting as I write about the polarity of Hank's father's rage and his softer side, how that is encapsulated in the historic and anthropological picture of man needing to be strong, competitive for fear that they will not just be overtaken by men, but they will not be able to really please, satisfy and do what their women and wives desire them to be. In 9/11 and other events like this throughout the ages, I can see on the surface, yet in reality solutions need not be so complicated. My friend Hank has done quite well solving his oedipal, aggression issues without giving up his power. Hank has taught me much over the years. Dedication, nonjudgment, true unconditional friendship, and strength. Hank is a winner and survivor.

As always, I was glad to see him, as I ate my delicious "but very expensive" Sunday brunch at the Crown Plaza Hotel in White Plains, New York waiting for him and his wife, Roberta, to pick me up. They were bringing me to their home in Ossining, New York where I would be staying during my trip to the New York area. Upon arriving in Ossining, we attended an evening church, multidenominational service for the victims of the World Trade Center attack. I saw some old buddies from High School. Doug McGrath was there. Doug and his two brothers, Larry and George, along with me, formed the first rock band that I was in, "The Swinging Pendulum." I think we had two or three jobs total. Probably made $10 a piece. Larry and George were always fighting. Inner band, male territorial aggression. Some things never change. They were all great guys nevertheless. Good friends. Doug reminded me of how I, as the drummer of the band, sang only one song, "Wooly Booly" by Hannibal and the Headhunters. Interesting, ironic name for a band, in view of my purpose in New York. We laughed a lot. Doug was now a CEO of a well-known psychiatric facility in Westchester County. I told him that as a result of my father's recent death, besides being a Psychologist, I had also just taken over his band in South Florida as the lead vocalist and new leader of the Tommy Mercer Orchestra, my other career on and off over the years and certainly a passion, "a part time endeavor that I have done intermittently since college." He asked me whether "Wooly Booly" was in my repertoire. We laughed. I always liked Doug. Seeing him was as if we had just finished one of our rehearsals in his garage so many years ago. For some reason, along with nostalgia, I felt sad. Tomorrow I would go into lower Manhattan.

Chapter II

I am sitting on the Express Commuter Train into New York City, as it speeds down the tracks toward Grand Central Station. I have not been on a New York train for many years. It is actually quite relaxing. I thought about how stressful it is living in South Florida, driving everywhere. Interesting how time changes your perspective. I used to think commuters into the city were robotlike nerds, bordering on androids. As the express (no stops at any station) travels, with the Hudson River to the right and towns like Irvington, Tarrytown, Dobbs Ferry and Yonkers, being passed by on the left, many boyhood memories begin to surface. I loved growing up in New York. The sleigh riding and "snow days" in the winter;

warm moonlight swimming parties; pick-up baseball games; the Good Humor trucks after high school; the sweet smell of spring as freshmen and Babe Ruth baseball began; playing the drums in the high school marching band on cold, fall afternoons at halftime; Christmas; family dinners; my grandfather; my Grandma Rosie; Priscilla Roe (man, I thought she was hot! I am not sure what she thought about me); My homeroom crush, gorgeous voluptuous Karen Mannage (who I recently hunted down in a high school "find a classmate" website) and admitted in an e-mail that she was always my fantasy; running the second leg in the 880 relay team; summers at Jones Beach, on the South Shore of Long Island; so many good memories. As the train pulls closer to Grand Central station in Manhattan, I wonder what my first day of trauma/debriefing counseling at a company titled Corporate Placement, Inc. (Fictitious name to protect identity of company), an executive search firm with offices on Wall Street and Park Avenue, would be like. I felt a little sad again. This experience was not and never will have the same positive fun-loving memories attached as the rest of those I had for New York. I am heading into a battlefield.

The lobby of Grand Central Station was bustling like any bustling Monday morning of any normal workweek in New York. I ask two police officers about the subway routes into lower Manhattan. They informed me there was no direct train to

Wall Street. I proceeded to get my ticket and take the #4 train to Fulton Street, not far from Wall Street. I happened to ask a young woman on the train the exact directions once I got off the subway and coincidentally, she was on her way to the same destination, "Trump Tower, 40 Wall Street." Ironically, that was my first stop. Donald Trump. A building named after himself. The ultimate capitalist. He probably represented the Western greed and arrogance that the terrorists despise, I thought to myself. I expressed my gratitude to this pretty professional woman, approximately twenty-eight years of age, for helping direct me through the maze of military and police checkpoints, armored vehicles, families, curious on-lookers and the grey dust that was still permeating the air in lower Manhattan. My new friend guided me toward Wall Street. She was actually a bit confused herself with the directions. The lofty landmarks, once reaching above the clouds were now reduced to rubble and could no longer be used as a reference point. The police barricades and impatient groups of military and paramilitary brought to this part of Manhattan a very different look. She was actually on the first day of a new job. I never did get her name. Beginnings and endings. Strange. Many of those stories abound in New York right now.

We came to a police checkpoint where they were inspecting ID's. I had to go through three officers before they would allow me to proceed forward.

Then I saw it. The remains of the World Trade Center. Like a postmodern sculpture rising into the sky. The jagged remains of what were once buildings over 1300 feet tall lay in the distance, enshrouded by "the cloud." I will try to gain more direct access to "ground zero" before I return to Florida. My friend, the young woman I had met on the Subway, was separated from me due to my delay in the police line. To my surprise, when I got to Trump Towers, she was waiting for me to see if I had found the building. What they say is not true; some New Yorkers are very friendly. For some reason, I felt compelled to bring her into the photo journal of my experience in New York. I took her picture. When the photograph was developed a few days later, I saw that look in her eyes that look of shock, sorrow, despair and bewilderment. Her facial countenance was universal for many New Yorkers both on that day and for days to come.

I took the elevator up to the forty-eighth floor and bid my friend farewell, wishing her good luck, not just with her first day on the job but in her own adjustments to the new life, which would certainly be characteristic of New York City. As I stepped out of the elevator on the forty-eighth floor, I approached the reception area of my first assigned business; I was ushered into my contact's office, Mr. Brillo. He actually first brought me to the individual whom I assume was the Chief Executive Officer of the company, but he appeared to be preoccupied on the phone and when he did look up in my direction, he appeared annoyed. Mr. Brillo in turn, brought me into his office. At that point, an executive coach came in to meet me. He was introduced by Mr. Brillo as a person on the staff with some counseling background, who wanted to know my procedure. I discussed my critical debriefing/adjustment disorder paradigm, but I suggested we might need to do some free flow debriefing work since this disaster had variables, which were unprecedented. After listening to me, this individual, who described himself as a coach, stated, "We are a pretty sophisticated group here." I wondered, humoring myself, was he referring to the top-dollar Wall Street costumes the clowns were wearing as opposed to my Burdines/J. C. Penney tweed sports-jacket and not perfectly manicured nails and hair? He did not really elaborate but I think he was implying that the staff would not need any basic introduction to fallout/symptoms of Post Traumatic Stress Disorder (PTSD). He was extremely affective as well as condescending. The ultimate was when the senior manager, who I had alluded to before, walked into the office and followed up the coach's comments with "I think people are doing pretty well. I appreciate you coming down, but I don't think we need to force our people into talking about this event." I looked at this individual and stated to him very directly that they may "appear all right now," but this kind of phenomenon often takes time, weeks, even months before symptoms appear. He said he realized that and then asked me my name. I repeated it, realizing he had not asked earlier and said it as if he did not really care about developing any kind of connection whatsoever. I thought to myself, this type of arrogance is what is found to fuel the despicable rage that certain fanatical groups have for Americans.

I was given my own office and Mr. Brillo stated that if anyone wanted to talk to me they could come here. I suspected this was just going through formality at this point. I was certain the message was loud and clear. Either they didn't like my tie and that I hadn't shaved that day due to no razors allowed on-board the flight up to New York, or this was a group, led by management, who quickly decided that I was being a bit too clinical and didn't want to get too serious with the staff and take their "competitive edge" away; maybe a combination of the two. Very odd, in that just the day before, I had been assigned to this company who had expressed a definite need for trauma counseling services. Denial and avoidance in action.

As I am sitting staring out the window of the small office that was "provided" to me, in case one of their employees actually did request counseling, I am listening to an obvious staff meeting being held down the hall full of laughter and applause. It is strange; it's as if these people are functioning in their own separate world, another reality. One would think that I would be introduced to the staff as I had suggested. But on this first morning of my assignment, I only felt sadness for those folks as I stared at the rubble not far from there. These are the arrogant New Yorkers. The hated, Western capitalistic, narcissistic Americans, whom these fanatical Muslims wish to eradicate. Fortunately, we Americans are not all alike. There are decent Westerners and decent Muslims. Even some of these Stepford people are decent, shallow but decent. I will be out of here very shortly, requesting an area in the five boroughs, in the surrounding area, where there is a true connection to the horrible reality that has and is unfolding in this city. I know my services are needed. Corporate Placement Inc., has been an experience that I did not anticipate. God help these pathetic, narrow, grandiose, self-righteous lives, and perceptions.

Chapter III

Understanding Severe Trauma

Let me take a moment to be a bit more specific about the condition of Post Traumatic Stress Disorder (PTSD) and its accompanying symptoms. It can take sometimes six months to one year for reactions to a traumatic episode to occur, sometimes even longer. Both physical and emotional symptoms are equally predominant. The individual may stay in a somewhat isolated or indifferent state of being for quite sometime and then develop acute pronounced symptoms. The following is a comprehensive list of symptoms to look for when assessing for PTSD, as well as a list of ways you can advise your clients as well as debrief yourself if you work as a critical incident therapist:

* American Red Cross Brief

Disasters create an abrupt change in reality. For thousands and thousands of people, reality now includes the loss of loved ones—spouses, partners, children, other relatives, friends, and neighbors.

For millions of people around the world connected to this tragedy only by media coverage, it means the loss of a measure of security and safety and a sense of vulnerability. For people who have already lived through disasters, this event brings back memories and emotions they had thought they had dealt with.

This information was prepared in order to help you recognize your feelings and physical symptoms, and to offer ways to reduce your stress and begin the healing process. Be assured that the following are very normal reactions to an abnormal event.

Common Reactions

- Shock, numbness, and disbelief that such a thing could happen.
- Fear concerning personal safety, the safety of loved ones, rescue personnel and the country as a whole.
- Grief for those who lost their lives and for those who are dealing with the aftermath of the destruction. Feelings of grief may be triggered

from losses suffered during World War II or any military action or response to terrorist activity, or any other type of violent event. Grieving is a natural outcome of such an event and may last for an extended period, especially when the event is still being discussed, and it's the subject of constant media coverage. The phrase "we are at war" contributes to this feeling.

- Flashbacks. Anyone who suffered PTSD from a previous incident may have the symptoms return. This is especially true of victims of violent acts, as I this circumstance; but it is also true for victims of domestic abuse and crime.

- Immediate anger, even rage, may be felt toward the specific human beings who hijacked the planes. This anger and suspicion can quickly become generalized toward others who are thought to me members of the same culture, nationality, and/or religion. Remember, we are still unsure of the identity of the people who conceived and initiated the attack and that they were individuals and do not represent everyone from their culture, their nation, or their faith.

- Survivor guilt is a feeling of "why am I alive" or "if only I had . . . "Belief in out ability to affect outcomes and to make a difference is a part of who we are. Types of survivor guilt include—

- Thinking that different behavior could have changed the outcome. People who were able to escape from the World Trade Center may feel they could have done more to save others.
- Worrying about unresolved issues with a person who died. The survivor focuses on guilty feelings about possible negligence, disagreements, misunderstandings, arguments, or unkind words. The survivor often feels that the person died without knowing he or she was loved.
- Feeling guilty and helpless because there was no opportunity to do anything. This is common to "secondary victims" (those who experienced the disaster only through the media) who feel helpless. This feeling is also common to search and rescue personnel who, if there were no survivors, had no opportunity to use their training and expertise.

• Feeling overwhelmed, having difficulty making decisions, and/or an inability to think clearly.

- Temporary memory loss, both short and long-term can be temporarily affected by sensory and information overload.
- Need to contact family members. There is a need to feel connected to those whom you love and who love you. The connection with your own support system is very important in managing your stress.
- Everyone is glued to their televisions and radios, hoping to hear that survivors have been found, and what the latest new is. Constant fixation on the event does not allow the body or mind to relax.
- Anxiety is different from fear. It is a general uneasiness or worry without any immediate realistic danger. Fear comes when there is an immediate and realistic threat.
- Depression is characterized by: crying for no apparent reason; frustration; feelings of powerlessness and hopelessness; irritability; isolating yourself from family and friends and/or social activities and a loss of self-esteem.

As a result of any or a combination of the above, you may experience: appetite changes; sleeping problems—most common is the inability to fall asleep or stay asleep; nightmares or you may also find that you are sleeping more; headaches; increased allergies and/or weight loss.

How You Can Help Yoursef and Others

o High levels of anxiety fueled by watching TV, listening to the radio, and reading about the disaster can be lowered by limiting your exposure to the sights and sounds of the disaster. This is probably the single most effective thing you can do at this time to help yourself.

o Focus on the positive. Remember that people of all nationalities, faiths, and cultures are standing with us.

o Recognize your own feelings. Talk to others about your feelings. Know that the physical and emotional problems you are having are stress related and that a shared experience helps reduce their effect on you.

o Accept help. If you need help putting your feelings in perceptive, talk to a mental health worker. They are trained in crisis intervention, and know that reactions of this type are normal.

o Deal with your anger, even against your will. Unresolved anger often turns into abuse against your family. Try some sort of physical activity or stress reducing techniques such as deep breathing exercises or meditation. Don't allow your anger to grow into hate.

o Offer to listen to others who need to talk. Reach out and embrace those who are being blamed for the acts of the terrorists just because they share a nationality or a religion. Their grief and pain is as great as yours. Do not condemn the many for the acts of the few.

o Whenever possible remember that you are still free and that there is still beauty in the world. It's OK to smile; it will make you feel better, and is in no way disrespectful.

o Stay in touch with your religious/spiritual leader, social groups, neighbors, family, and friends. Spend a night with a friend or family member. You can both benefit from the contact.

* The above reactions and suggestions are part of a document prepared by the Red Cross. Again, these can be used by the professional counselor and layperson alike when dealing with a traumatic disaster or event.

In evaluating how to present this particular tragedy to the corporate individual, I have to keep several facts in mind. First and foremost, this type of event is unprecedented. Therefore, there is no pure base line from which one can extrapolate data and use for developing a relevant treatment plan. Civilians in our country, on our soil were directly assaulted and many lost their lives. We saw the attack and the subsequent collapse of the Twin Towers on television as it happened and then that footage was repeated over and over and over again. I broke the event down into levels of intensity, from the most severe potential traumatic reaction to the least. They are as follows: (and remember this is designed specifically for this catastrophe and could be applied to similar events in the future)

1) Experienced the direct loss of loved one, i.e., wife, husband.
2) Experienced a direct loss of friend/colleague/co-worker.
3) Suffered a serious personal injury.
4) Witnessed jumpers/body parts/deceased from the attack.
5) Directly viewed/witnessed attacks and collapse of buildings.
6) Viewed it on television.
7) Had been in similar experience, i.e., hijacking.
8) Had experienced loss of loved one in a similar experience/event.
9) Going through acute distress or loss, i.e., depression/death of parent and symptoms exacerbate.
10) Fear of being in buildings near Ground Zero or in Manhattan in general.

Along with this, I included the stages one might expect to go through as they deal with this event over months to come. Reactions include shock, denial, depression, anger, and bartering, which are similar to the stages one passes through in the normal grieving process. I suspected, however, there would be some very new responses to this multifaceted event and there definitely were, including my own difficulty, emotionally in taking in and absorbing the massive amount of trauma reported to me in these five days. Little did I know, as I conducted CISD interviews and consultations, that I would be taking back to South Florida, the remnants of the buildings, the deceased and most of all the horrific recall of the victims, who will hold these images within their subconscious, to be lifted out, all too often for the reminder of their lives.

Chapter IV

Question of Closure

After leaving Corporate Placement Inc., I took advantage of being free from contract work until the following day. I attempted to get into the apex of Ground Zero, but was met with stiff opposition from local police agencies. NYPD had strict orders to keep just about everyone out of the actual attack/search and rescue area. My professional credentials and my purpose for being in New York made no difference. I was not allowed to get any closer than two blocks away. What I saw from this distance was shocking nevertheless. In the cloud-enshrouded distance, you could see the steel monument with its jagged edge pointing to the sky, surrounded by the remains and rubble that was once the Twin Towers. It looked like a movie set from Steven Spielberg. It wasn't. This was very real. It didn't hit me until later, that

the gray ash that seemed to cover the surrounding
debris in the area, that had covered all people and
things on the day of attack, was not just what was left
of the pulverized concrete, but in a sense of reality
almost too much to comprehend, this gray ash was
also the cremated remains of thousands of victims
who perished in the attacks, explosions, and fires.

I walked uptown from Ground Zero to catch a
subway to the Plaza Hotel where I would be doing
some counseling with families and victims from
another company, but I was feeling numb. I was
feeling so numb that I passed right by a New York
pizza vendor and didn't even buy a slice. For those
who know my fondness for New York pizza, this
was a somewhat stark illustration that I was indeed
preoccupied in this moment.

I took the subway to a stop in Midtown. I got off
and walked several blocks to the Plaza Hotel where
Cantor and Fitzgerald, a brokerage firm that had
lost seven hundred of one thousand employees, was
having a volunteer support therapy day. I decided
to go and lend my services since my afternoon
assignment, the uptown branch of Corporate
Placement, was scratched.

The Plaza is an elegant hotel, one of the finest
in the city. As the harp player ushered me into the
lobby, I proceeded to the main ballroom where the
counseling services for the families and friends of
the victims was being held. I was given a name tag
and was told that the format went as follows: Don't

be too pushy, just go up to a person, identify yourself, and see if they have a need to talk. If they don't have a need, move on. In the same breath, I was told not to just "hang out" and eat the free lunch (My friends and family would have gotten a good laugh from that remark—I have quite the appetite). It seemed as if the volunteer professional counselor needed to exercise a sort of humility and very reticent approach in identifying who wanted to discuss their feelings.

I rescanned the enormous ballroom that Howard Cantor, one of the owners of the firm has leased for the counseling. I sat down with one group. It turned out they were the three brothers (including his twin) and the wife of one of the men who worked at Cantor who was missing.

They were part of a very large German-Irish Catholic family of thirteen children. I just listened to each as they spoke of Jim, the missing brother/husband who was presumed dead. They had no body, no remains, and no closure. One brother, a handsome man in his early fortie's, asked me whether it was too early to have a memorial service. I said, follow your heart. The wife of the man who had perished was in a predepressive manic state, not an unusual phase at this very early juncture of such a loss. I made a comment to myself; there is no real true rhyme or reason for procedure here. I think just my presence and my listening ear was sufficient. This was not the arena for profound therapeutic interpretation. This was a place of unfathomable grief. I bid them farewell. I felt especially sad for the remaining twin. He had truly lost a part of himself. More than likely he would have to move on without ever having total psychological or physical closure with his dead brother and best friend. The one good thing regarding this particular family was that it was large, providing an extensive support network of caring, nurturing, and sustaining individuals. People need people in times of strife and conflict. The tragedy of 9/11 has taken the American public to a place it has never seen, nor experienced. A place of dread, death, and destruction. This Irish family had each other. They were fortunate. For this evil death struck others with more savagery, more malevolence. The 9/11 left some individuals, children and adults alike, totally alone in the world. It had no mercy. One gentleman, sitting alone at a table, lost in his grief over a loved one, simply waved me on, as if he were motioning to a corner news boy hawking a Sunday paper. He was not ready to talk. Shock was his only companion. I quietly informed him that I would be there for him if he needed or wanted to talk. He had nothing to say. Nothing to spare. His sad, disbelieving eyes said it all. I suspected he had lost his wife. Gender was not a determinant for the loss of life on this battlefield. To this day, there is a significantly higher proportion of male infantry fighting on the front lines of our wars than female. The 9/11 and its battlefield was different, men and women perished equally, leaving widows and widowers alike.

Chapter V

Day 3

September 18, 2001

The morning began in Queens, New York. My assignment today was to do debriefing/trauma counseling on Queens Blvd., at a Chase Bank office and in the afternoon head out to Long Island to do the same with a different branch of the same company. After spending the first night in Westchester with Hank and Roberta, I had decided to drive down and station myself in the Manhattan area for the next couple of days. I anticipated that the stress that would accompany taking trains and subways to various locations would put me on overload and Roberta was kind enough to lend me her car to do my work here. We had dinner with her parents that night. The mood was somber. It was surrealistic being back in my hometown after such a long absence. How simple and predictable life in a small town is. Good people, warm, kind, uncomplicated people. I had departed many years ago to search for my Holy Grail. Was that search and 9/11 leading me back to Kansas? I wondered as we ate pasta, sipped wine and puzzled over the events that would change even this simple place forever.

The morning was uneventful at the Queens location. There were only about four employees in the Queens branch. I spoke to one manager and did a crisis counseling phone call to an employee who was too shaken to come to work and then proceeded to drive out to an area near Valley Stream, Long Island: Rockville Center. This was where, to the ringing of banking telephones answering requests regarding the status of loans, as business went on as usual, I would be brought into the hell of 9/11.

The Long Island branch of this company was an entirely different story. This was my first real test as a critical incident specialist for 9/11. I ran a group with a female co-therapist, Olga. She was a Latin gal, very New York, probably Brooklyn born, tough, to the point, no B.S. I liked her style. The range of emotions was significant: anger, fear, and confusion. One man had lost three neighbors. As he spoke during the round-table group discussion, therapy session, he wept, as did others. Another man had been at Ground Zero with a male co-worker who was also in this therapy group. Brian, the latter, was very expressive with his feelings and wonderfully articulate, as he described the chaos that followed the first airliner striking Tower 1. He saw people jump. This experience went beyond words. He (Brian) became suddenly numb, stoic, almost rigidly catatonic-like. He paused for almost twenty seconds and as his face turned more and more crimson, he finally, after what seemed like an eternity, blurted "I can't talk right now. I'm sorry;" He put his head down and sobbed.

The "jumpers." I referred to this earlier. The defiant ones. Not suicidal in the least. Lovers of life. Aggressive in both business and their personal pursuit of the adrenalin high. Rock climber, black diamond powder moguls, white water. These would not wait for the flames. These "jumpers," unlike the suicidal man jumping to his final destination onto the hotel lobby floor with no reason or desire to live, had many more plans and many more mountains to conquer. They were by no means suicidal. On the contrary, in some mystical, magical way, I'm sure some of them, perhaps the couple caught in so many news camera lenses, holding hands as they descended from the window ledge of a 101st floor window, believed they were actually still asleep in a hypnotic, pre awakening state, back in Jersey or Staten Island or Westchester, before they had their cheerios or morning kisses goodbye. Their kiss goodbye for the last time was like a strange, time-warp trigger, and by jumping, they would suddenly just be back in bed with just a passing thought about that "bad dream". (I smile for some unknown reason as I recall their ghostly image; "Back damn death, you will not take me without a fight." God bless their souls. Shit, I am still so f*&-#g angry about what took place on that day!)

Brian saw the couple land; hitting the concrete pavement below with such force that he recalled nothing, absolutely nothing resembling a human being laying there identifiable. Land. Land again. One "jumper" after another. He said at one point it was like a human hail storm of bodies seemingly falling from the sky. Some tragically landing on other office workers from the Twin Towers, themselves trying to run from the carnage, never making it to safety. Killed suddenly by falling debris. Not pieces of cement or metal, but debris of flesh and blood of our American sisters and brothers. Falling arms, legs, torsos; falling, plummeting, rocketing human shrapnel. He just laid his head again in his forearms on the table and sobbed. I cried for the first time of my debriefing work in New York City as Brian wept for the "jumpers." I cried for them. I hope my tears, his tears never dry, they need to flow, creating a new river of hope and pride. Flowing from a river of remembrance, a river that cuts its way throughout our eternal memory of this event. We cannot forget them.

The "jumpers" or Brian on 9/11. We cannot forget them. We cannot forget 9/11.

Vince, the other gentleman, was a Sylvester Stallone look-alike. He fit the profile exactly, tough, emotionless male. Tough guy. Summarily, he described himself as being fine. I felt for him as I did the Stepford men from Corporate Placement Inc. They will all feel this pain. It will not dismiss anyone. As I listened to the ten staff members discuss their respective experience of 9/11, my heart felt heavy, their road of healing was just beginning.

On an anecdotal level, just to sidetrack for a bit, as I write down my own accounts of this tragedy to human kind, I feel the need to detach myself from my own emotions. This type of counseling is not easy. It is not for everyone. I have the temperament for it. If you are a therapist and want to do major trauma/debriefing interventions, examine all the variables. I myself will look for bright, tiny openings that radiate warmth and humor when I do debriefing work. There are always positive experiences, even in the worst of times. One of these was tonight, as I jump ahead, sitting at the bar of my hotel, eating a late dinner and trying to wind down. I was drinking a Coca Cola. The bartender, a fast talking Latino gal, was talking to two male patrons sitting next to me. One gentleman was Caucasian, the other, African-American. I am setting the stage multi-culturally; because heritage and gender play a significant role in determining human behavior and more importantly, how we may thus perceive and react to that behavior. We had certainly been witnesses as the clash of religious/cultural dogmas took a new twisted turn that past week during and after 9/11. It is often our subjective and socially shaped perceptions which lead to distorted comprehension and too often, ill fated judgment.

Back to the scene at the bar: They were obviously regulars. One was discussing in a very provocative manner, and in earshot of the attractive, Latin bartender, about how his girlfriend just had his baby (even though this gentleman discussed his wife in the same breath). The bartender let him know in a kind, but firm way, that he would last about as long as it takes her to mix a martini, if he behaved this way as her husband (or boyfriend). The other gentleman, a good-looking African American, responded to her by saying, "any man would be a fool to cheat on you." She did not hear this remark. I almost echoed his validation to her, but decided to leave its reference to the collective unconsciousness. The bartender was a wise woman.

Chapter VI

Day 4

I had decided to stay in Queens one more night, even though my next assignment was, according to what I had been told, going to be Pearl River, which is actually across the Tappanzee Bridge just a little south from Ossining, where I was staying with my friends, on the other side of the Hudson River and Rockland County. But, as fate would have it, amidst the confusion and chaos that had spread like the waves of nuclear fallout after an atomic blast, communication was not always totally accurate this week between agencies and consultants like me. So when I received my assignment from the Chicago office, which contracted me saying that I would be at Pearl River (North of New York City), mistakenly I received, from that same office, the name of the chief director of the Hoboken, New

Jersey (directly across the Hudson River from Manhattan) subdivision of North American Express and not Pearl River. Since I really didn't put two and two together at that moment (I didn't differentiate between Pearl River and Hoboken), I just assumed that since this was the contact person's name and number that she'll give me directions and I'll go up to my next assignment.

Upon awaking on Day three, in my hotel on Queens Blvd, I called up my contact person and she gave me directions as to how to navigate through the Holland Tunnel and over to the other side of the Hudson into Jersey where her office was. As I was making my way over there and I ended up being stranded in traffic at the entrance of the tunnel for at least one hour. It began to hit me that my original instructions did have me going to Pearl River. I remember them saying that it was across the Tappanzee and near Nyack and I thought, hmmm, this is certainly not across the Tappanzee or near Nyack, but I dismissed the thought with the knowledge that I was just following directions and on my way to what I thought was my next assignment.

Upon arriving in Hoboken, I got somewhat lost in finding the new North American Express office. I called their number and a young man came to the gas station (7-Eleven) that I had pulled over to. It was actually right across the street from the office. He jumped in my car and brought me to the site.

As we walked up the stairs, I assumed that this firm had been in this office for quite some time, and that they were just moving into a new space in the building. Having not received any major debriefing as far as each individual site, I had to use my own imagination regarding certain details. We arrived upstairs to the North American Express office, and it was clear that construction was still going on. I still assumed that they were just moving into a new part of the building, but eventually, I learned they were moving into this building for the first time. Their entire office, which they had occupied for years, had been destroyed in the attack on the Twin Towers. Due to the extreme shock which had befallen these individuals, as it had done to so many hundreds of thousands of New Yorkers on that fateful day, people were numb, frozen in time, emotions suspended, functioning like mechanical robots. As a result, their standard cognitive skills were also suspended, or at least impaired. Therefore, communication, which in normal situations would be a given, was not taking place. Ergo, I found out through my own gradual assimilation of information that these poor souls, who had witnessed the worst carnage of human life to ever occur on our soil, were forced to pack their bags and move to a new office miles from daily business, as if it were any cool day in September.

As the senior manager rounded up employees to participate in a debriefing group therapy session, it became apparent that everybody in the room had been in Tower 1 when the first plane hit, had escaped, but as they discussed, had seen abomination of human nature. As each person spoke about their pain, either sitting on the uncarpeted floor or standing up, as we used a room that was not yet furnished, my heart went out to each and everyone in the room. They had all escaped physically unharmed, but had seen the "jumpers," had lost friends, had been displaced, not because of a corporate move, but because of terrorist attacks upon their "second home," as one young woman put it. Some of the employees had been in their Manhattan offices for years. Emotions again ranged from grief, sadness, anger, and rage. I covered them as best as I could during my debriefing, and I said to them that they need to comfort each other every day and at least one day a week have a special group, just to support each other's emotions. I asked the senior manager how she was doing, and she replied, "Oh, I'm doing OK." She reminded me a bit of the standoffish, aloof, arrogant, Wall Street type that I had dealt with earlier in the week. She did not have the pomposity that he did, but she certainly had the denial of the magnitude of the situation.

Just like the Wall Street androids, she will also eventually melt down. It may take one day, one week, or one month, but she will melt down. Her frozen affect and feelings will unfreeze. She will be an emotional tidal wave, probably like nothing she ever experienced. Some of these employees of this particular company were already manifesting signs of their personal beaches being enveloped and eroded by the surging waves of grief and trauma. Some, like the manager, were better defended, their walls were up, but for anyone who has ever experienced high storm surge, the beach is always the loser. I would try my best to help them prepare for the long restoration of their personal beaches, one grain of sand at a time.

Chapter VII

Day 5

September 20, 2001

My last day of debriefing/trauma counseling, took place in a town called Pearl River, in Upstate New York. It lays across the Hudson, nestled in the hills of Rockland County, a small little town, very unassuming, unpretentious. I checked into a Holiday Inn the night before, after having finished the remainder of my trauma counseling at another of the subdivision offices of American Express, the company branch that I had been assigned to at their new Hoboken, New Jersey office. As I sat at the bar at the hotel drinking my usual Coke, just watching the television reports of the attack and other related events, the bartender, an older gentleman, made a comment about the footage of the Afghanistan village that was on CNN. It showed Afghan women and children, looking very scared, tired, depleted, and very nonthreatening. This man, bartender, probably in his mid to late sixties, appearing like a very patriotic Republican-type, showed an unusual amount of sensitivity especially toward the children in the footage. He said how horrible it was, them (the U.S. military) bombing this country, all these children are going to be dying. I agreed and thought about how ludicrous all of this conflict was. How senseless, how insane, how utterly devastating, and most of all, how hopeless. It's interesting, as I sit here and dictate, speaking into my mini recorder, people must feel I'm an undercover Marshall or Police Officer. Everybody has a little paranoia, hyper-vigilance. I can't really blame them. Post Traumatic Stress Syndrome has certainly already set in to the culture up here. I expect over the next six months to a year that random acts of heightened violence between each other, between citizens will occur. Below my hotel window the other night in Queens, during my counseling assignment there, as I was stationed at companies both in Queens and Rockville Center, Long Island, I heard a commotion downstairs. I looked out my window and observed what appeared to be a road rage episode where a man had been cut off by another driver. I didn't see the whole thing, but apparently he stopped the other car, pulled the driver out, screamed at him and said, "you mother f—ing asshole, first

you call me an asshole then you turn your back!"
Immediately after that I heard three or four thumps
as if somebody was being banged up against a car.
I couldn't make out the entire situation, but it
sounded ugly, nasty. I wondered whether this was
just the typical road rage aggressive episode that
we hear about so often, mostly with men who are
angry and frustrated and take out their anger with
vehicular rage, or whether this was a beginning
statement, an omen, to what lies ahead. The result
of the aggression and reconstruction that all the
New Yorkers of this area were direct victims of,
whether they were in the Twin Towers, watching it
collapse as they stood on a nearby street or working
in uptown Manhattan when the attack occurred. All
have been impacted for life. As the bartender and I
talked, we watched the children, beautiful children
sadness was shared between us both. This man
of a different generation than mine, of different
political values and beliefs more than likely, but
nevertheless we had one commonality, and that was
our despicable distaste for what was going on in our
world. Maybe that's one consolation. The events of
the past days have brought people together who
normally wouldn't come together. Maybe it won't
all be in vain, this horrible loss of life. Maybe it will
raise up some type of bonding effect for Americans.
I hope so, but I have some doubt. Americans are
as a whole, a very narcissistic, self-involved group
of human beings. Spoiled by the ease we have

with attainment of creature comforts and luxury, items which few other countries enjoy. We tend to obsess with "who has more and how much." We are a reactive society whether it is the stock market, impulsive spending, or anger. I'm not sure whether one event or series of events will have a dramatic impact on an overall pervasive cultural change. But we can hope nevertheless.

As I drove to my training site, on this seasonably chilly morning, it was a typical dreary, rainy, early fall day in New York, the kind of weather that makes me feel glad that I live in Florida. I don't like cold and rainy days. Not unless I am inside, relaxing and enjoying someone I care about. These are not days to be on the road driving. Fortunately, I did not have too far to drive from my hotel. I found the location of the new North American Express Office, far removed from the Twin Towers, where they had been for 15 to 20 years, but now found themselves in, what one employee referred to as, "the boondocks in upstate New York." Being the only high rise building in the whole town, it was a rather large office complex. I walked through the doors and took an elevator upstairs to the second floor where the North American Express office was located. I was brought in to meet the Office Manager, Don, a pleasant, somewhat overweight man in his mid forties. I introduced myself and said I was here as the assigned trauma specialist. He had a kind of blank look in his eyes, more than likely dazed from the attack, the repercussions, the relocation to this new office, the stress on his employees, and more than anything else, for the first time in their twenty years of marriage, Don and his wife were forced to be apart. It wasn't because they were going through midlife marital strife and were electing to put some distance in between their stagnant, predictive lives. On the contrary, it was only when Don began talking to me about his wife that the blank, lifeless eyes suddenly found life again. He elaborated to me that he now had enormous responsibilities as captain of his ship since the 9/11 fall out. He was forced to make a difficult decision once his office was relocated to up the Hudson River about two hours north of Manhattan, where the Twin Towers had once majestically rose. This everyday man lived with his beloved wife and two children, across the river from lower Manhattan in New Jersey. It would take him at least the same two hours to drive to his new location from his home every morning, and that was now. This was September in New York. The weather had a little chill in the air but two months from now, the chill would become a prewinter cold that would beckon a rain-turned-to-ice glaze on the roads making driving very hazardous and thus, if one wished to make it to work in one piece, driving time would be even longer with the slower speeds. And then winter's snow would fall, and fall it would, especially in the hilly countryside where his new office was located.

Consequently Don had to make a decision, one that both he and his wife of twenty loving years knew they had to make. If he was to keep his stress level down during these extremely stressful days and weeks to come he had to simplify his existence. He had to arrive at work every morning now and not be just the manager of his staff, but a sensitive and supportive one. For Don knew what was in store. The tension was already beginning to erupt in short tempers and words, which one could not take back. Two of his favorite middle managers got into it the other day. They were best friends and never had an ill word to say about one another. But now everything was different. It would never go back to the way it was. The savages flying those planes into the Towers on 9/11 not only demolished thousands of lives in the matter of minutes but also managed to send a shockwave that no matter how intense was moving at a snail's pace. Don knew this shockwave would reach the psychological crevices of his staff eventually and when it did, he would have to be there for them in every sense of the word. So Don, with the support and encouragement of his senior superiors, did something that he never in a million years ever conceived he would do. He moved out of his home into an apartment only two miles from his new office but two hours plus from his home and the one person in the world he needed now more than ever.

As Don spoke of this necessary weekly separation from his wife and kids, that blank, distant stare that was becoming so characteristic of many of the New Yorkers who I was counseling, came back to Don's countenance, accompanied by something new—sadness in his eyes. Don had not once shown me this entirely normal human emotion as he spoke about his thoughts regarding the Twin Towers attack and the horrible aftermath. Until now, his eyes were not only sad; but tears were welling up in them as he spoke about the practical, logical, safer, good-for-the-company, and devastating decision that he had to make—being away from the only truth and sanity that existed in this now seemingly-gone-mad world. He stated to me that his wife was fully understanding and supportive as she always had been and he counted the minutes, as the end of his last day of each work week approached, so he could go home for the weekend to those who, for a short time at least, could make the horror disappear from his mental imagery. I thanked Don for his time and stated that I would be available throughout the day if he needed to talk. He said he appreciated that, but added he doubted that even if he did experience the need to process some unnerving, interfering thought of emotion, he would not have time.

His name was Don, one of the many special, courageous souls I encountered during these days of September, and by the end of the day, he was very grateful that I was there, as were most of his employees. I was grateful that I was there also to help them during these acutely tough times, and for me to learn about the true meaning of strength. They were just as much my teachers as I was theirs.

All I can say is; these poor souls. I spoke in front of the entire staff of this North American Express office (fictitious name), which was comprised of thirty some odd people. I introduced myself and told them why I was here and what I had planned for the day. We'd break off into small groups and they would just share with me and among themselves their feelings, emotions, and reactions to the recent events. The stories were many. Certainly as was the theme of the week, in all my training, the biggest impact was for those who had been at Ground Zero at the time of the first plane hitting the building. Running down the stairs, being outside amidst falling debris and falling bodies. Many people throughout the days training, broke down as they spoke of watching people deliberately jump from 80, 90 floors up, to their certain death. One young man, a Manager at North American Express, probably about thrity-two, thirty-three years of age, recalled with tears in his eyes that he remembers the first two "jumpers," as New Yorkers have learned to refer to them as. He

remembers the first "jumper," was a man wearing a
red shirt and Levis; and the second, another man,
obviously an Executive, was wearing a blue power
suit. Status, position, ethnic background, nationality,
gender, none of these applied to this random act
of violence. I think every nationality, approximately
60 different nations, represented the victims, more
than 6000* of them now, who are still missing and
certainly deceased from the blast. This was not an
attack on just one population, just Americans, but
on every culture. I have been using the metaphor
that came up in one of the training sessions on Long
Island all week when one of the men said, who was
at the blast site, as he watched everybody running
who were consumed and enveloped by the cloud
of gray smoke, dust, asbestos: Their color was gray.
Everyone was gray. There were no nationalities,
ethnic color tones, only gray. Suddenly, we were all
one. There was no distinction. I said to the group,
"Maybe that's one good thing that came from this.
Maybe we can use this incident to unite us more, to
break down racial and ethnic barriers and be the
same color metaphorically."

I warned them of the rage and the anger that is
more likely going to hit them at different times and
the potentiality of displacement of this anger, not an
unusual reaction to post traumatic stress disorder
and certainly because of how unprecedented this
is, the potential is awesome. I warned them not
to generalize their anger toward Middle-Eastern

people as a whole. There have already been reports of random acts of violence, again, against Middle-Eastern people in the New York City area. There are also reports, disgusting as it may seem, of local New York and New Jersey, Middle-Eastern people celebrating the bombings in public, in bars, on the streets. One of those people was chased down by a group of non-Middle-Eastern Americans and shot. It's very scary up here. I do not like it.

The training throughout the day was very successful at Pearl River. The group shared their feelings, their sadness, their pain, and their anger. We held each other, people cried. One woman only sleeps two hours a day. Others reported a variety of acute physical symptoms such as headaches, insomnia, loss of appetite, loss of libido (sex drive), etc. All were still in the very early stages of post-traumatic disorder (actually at this juncture, it was more of an adjustment disorder) and their symptoms were certainly

* This number has been estimated to be considerably lower since the writing of this book

going to increase in intensity as time went on. One young man stands out in my mind. He actually had decided not to go to work at his job at North American Express on September 11. Rather, he stayed at home to help his wife prepare their five-year-old son for his first day at school. This is his story.

Chapter XIII

He was an Ashkenazi Jew from South Africa. She, Lena, his wife, was a Sephardic Jew from Turkey. They had a son, Damon, age two. Victor, Damon's father and Lena's husband was actually born in the States but moved to South Africa, when he was four, with his parents. He lived there from ages four through fifteen. He witnessed the atrocities and oppression of Apartheid. His young mind, he recalled, had difficulty comprehending the inhumanity that he witnessed, sometimes on a daily basis. Man's torment and total disdain for fellow man, just because of race and creed. He, the young Victor could never understand the cruelty. Especially the one memory. The bad one. The one that never leaves his cerebral cortex. The one that haunts him like a ghost ship drifting in the dark sea. In Johannesburg, as his eyes looked off into a direction far from this world, he recalled the police standing over a man who they had just severely beaten. Crouching down and wiping the blood from his daddy's brow was a little boy, the man's son, probably no more than three, four years at the most. Victor remembers the look on the little boy's face as his father lay in the street gravely injured; his head the size of a basketball, from the beating. That look of total hopelessness was the same look he saw on the faces of the nameless masses who walked the streets of lower Manhattan, covered with the gray ash, but whose eyes could still peer out. Victor also lived in Israel for some years before he returned to the States to build a successful import-export business. He had seen violence there (Israel) as well. He always had a feeling that one day there was going to be a major event. An event that was fostered by the rabid hatred for both Israel and the States. An event that would not only shake the ground we stand on but the fiber of freedom that we thought was wound very tightly. So when 9/11 took place and sent the Twin Towers tumbling down like all the kings' horses and men, he was not surprised. Having felt the intensity of the hate that is spawned by those who would choose to see America as such exist no more, he knew the day would come.

Victor was one of the several spouses who I had the privilege to work with during my assignment to counsel the direct victims of 9/11. His wife was quite tight-lipped and did not want to recall the horrible events of the fateful day in September. She stated she was utilizing the spirituality she had learned as a little girl growing up in Turkey, to pull her through. She did not believe in the therapy or counseling process as a whole. She did honor, however, her husband's desire to talk about his recollection of the morning of 9/11. She did say during the group counseling session, which included other spouses as well, that she was worried about Victor. He had not been himself since that late Indian summer morning in the year 2001. He reflected only several weeks before; he and his wife decided they would move from the Upper East Side of Manhattan down to Battery Park in the southern end of the city. The school district there was the best and they only wanted the best for their son who would start kindergarten on September 11, the first day of his new school and long school career. Little did they know the other milestone event that their son's special day, his first day in school, would be over shadowed by.

Victor recalls feeling so excited about the prospect of living in lower Manhattan. It was indeed one of the prime areas for a young urban couple to reside. Their apartment was beautiful. Its kitchen window had an awesome view of the gigantic monolith that stood proud not too far a distance from their dwelling. The Twin Towers were certainly impressive and majestic. He looked forward to the routine of eating breakfast and starting his workday as he stared at their power and all they represented about freedom to raise to the highest peak of your individual potential. He liked America. It had been good, very good to his young family.

Lena had taken the day off on September 11. She would take one of the many sick days that she was entitled to in her middle management corporate position. Victor remembered how proud he was of her as he watched her walk down the hallway of their building taking Damon to his first day at school. Fifteen minutes later his world changed forever. It was no longer a perfect, clear, sunny September morn. Evil had interrupted the beauty. Victor recalled looking out his kitchen window when he heard the engines of the jet passing all too close to the skyline. He saw it as the jet, at full throttle slammed into the first of the Towers, leaving a gaping hole with confetti-like paper flying in every direction. He thought how ironic that office paper that looked like confetti, the stuff they use to honor heroes as they pass by in a parade of celebration and accomplishment, was one of the first images which imprinted t he minds of millions on that dark day. It was the anti thesis of celebration. It was a party for the devil.

Seconds after the hole, came the fiery explosion and flames that engulfed the side of the Tower. Panic set in. Victor had no idea as to the safety or whereabouts of his wife and child. Had they made it to the school, were they trapped somewhere on the street with the growing crowd? Victor was beside himself with grief. He remembers collapsing on the floor of his kitchen for an undetermined length of time, sobbing. He composed himself and as soon as he did the other jet crashed into the other Tower. He looked out the window again and he could not believe his eyes. Both Towers were now engulfed in their top portions by flames and thick smoke began to spew. And then the unspeakable. Victor heard a loud rumbling sound. One of the Towers began to cave in and suddenly the entire gigantic structure which took years and many hard man-hours to erect, collapsed within seconds. About the time it takes to cross a not-so-busy two-lane street, the entire structure just came crashing to the ground, with thousands of people inside and below on the street. He was sick with worry. Where were his wife and child? He had to go find them.

Victor got on his bike downstairs and it was at this point that the monster, the giant monster of ash and dust came rolling down the street as if to wipe out everything in its path. Victor just made it into a store to escape the evil cloud. His mind was somewhat "fuzzy" at this point, he stated, but he was determined to find his family—alive. As he rode his bike uptown, he momentarily looked up to see dark objects falling from the remaining tower. He shuddered. They were bodies. Human bodies, hurling themselves out of windows to fall to a certain death. He could not bear to watch. Why would anyone do this? But he could not know what goes on in the mind and heart of one when he or she is faced with certain death. He could not even begin to conjecture what the conditions were like for those poor souls, sons, daughters, husbands, wives, as they lived their final seconds. Maybe jumping was the final proactive, self-determined gesture that they would make. Almost like a "screw you" to those responsible for this evil deed. At least they who chose to jump wanted to be as much a part of their ultimate fate on that sunny, now gray morning in September, as they could. They weren't going to wait for death to come to them. They were going to take it and the terrorists on, head first. They chose to go to their death in one final moment of the freedom and independence that the Twin Towers stood for, that this country is founded on, and which will prevail over time.

Victor eventually reunited with his wife and Damon in Greenwich Village. A kind woman had taken them in. Lena had borrowed her cell phone to call Victor to let him know they were safe. As the debriefing group was coming to an end Victor added one final anecdotal memory chunk. As he and his family rode the subway uptown to stay with a friend, an older gentleman sitting across from them on the subway car, suddenly turned purple and was gasping for breath. Victor remembers the conductor coming to his aid and signaling for the train to stop and called for medics at the next station. Unfortunately, before help could arrive, the man drifted into unconsciousness and died. He died right in front of Victor, Lena, and Damon. Died. He should have been much more shaken to witness such an event. But Victor recalled that he was just numb. He didn't want Damon to look but he himself was numb. A situation that normally would have been extremely upsetting prior to 9/11 was now just a blemish on the face of the world, which had already changed just in the few hours since the first plane hit. The man's death was sad but it paled in comparison to the loss and horror that consumed lower Manhattan as he and his family walked off the train to start a new life with many questions and no answers.

Chapter IX

On top of the reaction to the events surrounding 9/11, there was another impacting variable that had the Pearl River employees stressed and unnerved. It was the fact that now, instead of traveling to the Twin Towers from their prospective homes, they have to travel every day, many miles north across the Hudson River, where there is no mass transit. These are people all of whom do not drive. They relied for many years on mass transit to take them from their homes on Staten Island, Long Island, Brooklyn, and Queens to lower Manhattan. Now, there is no mass transit. There are no Twin Towers, they have been reduced to rubble. These people's lives changed so dramatically that they not only had to deal with their feelings, their visions and their images of the burning buildings and the people falling and jumping, but they also had to deal with their feelings of anger and disgust for their corporate situation. That their lives have been made a multitude times more difficult with the new office location. So incredibly far away. I particularly empathized with them in that I grew up in the, oftentimes, difficult, frigid temperatures of upstate New York. The fall brings cold, rainy and treacherous driving conditions with the later autumn nights too often slipping below freezing leaving an invisible, but deadly transparent layer of ice on the roads. The winter months. Let's just say you are fortunate if all the driving for work that you do is to the local rail station to hop onto the commuter train to the city. Otherwise on the snow-drifted lined streets with the invisible layer of ice covering the pavement, negotiating a city block can feel like forever.

The employees in the Pearl River office knew what was to come. The drive to and from work in the cold days of fall and winter could be a dangerous, long, and arduous ordeal. One manager is responsible for driving five employees everyday. He lives in Staten Island. He has to pick up several employees and drive to Pearl River. He is on the road for approximately 6 hours everyday, on top of his 10 or 12-hour workday. That comes out to be about 18 hours on the job, with another 6 hours to combine sleeping, eating, and recreation. Need I go any further? This manager specifically told me during a debriefing session that if something isn't done, even though he is the guy who takes care of business, he is always in control; he is going to lose control. He looked at me with a look that combined both, pleading, anger, and desperation. This is a tough guy, a tough New Yorker, who had worked his way up into a system and was doing quite well in life, and all of a sudden, he was not in control any longer and he was angry about it. He was angry with his manager, Don, the nice guy. He was angry at the corporate structure. He was angry with the suicidal lunatics who commanded the planes of 9/11. He was just plain angry and scared. I told him that I would be making recommendations to the top brass. That my position here was certainly to help people ventilate and to identify their feelings, but equally as important, if not more important, was to make recommendations to these companies for interventions and procedures that may well save their employees from taking a major emotional dive bomb from the impact of the attacks, the relocation of offices, the loss of life, and the general subsequent stress involved.

I sat down with Don, the manager, at the end of the day. He was very thankful that I was there. He agreed with all my recommendations. I said that I would be giving a proposal to his top brass. I saw two things predominantly necessary right off the bat. Number one, even though they had an EAP program that provided counseling, which I thought everyone needed to investigate, the EAP program would only give them a limited number of sessions and number two, these people had no time for therapy, literally. Between driving, working, and everyday fundamentals, they're lucky if they can find time to catch three meals a day. I said to Don, this is a bomb ready to blow. Not an explosive physical bomb, but one of a psychological nature. He agreed with me. He was dealing with his own internal turmoil, silently, denouncing any emotions that even faintly spoke of weakness in his mind, that he was OK, that his wife was feeling it more than he. As previously explained, Don decided to stay in a hotel, so that he would not have to drive five days a week. He said his wife cried about this decision. There would be many more tears to come.

This attack is disrupting families, marriages, creating orphans. I vacillate between rage, anger, and just a deep sadness for everything that I have seen and heard. When I get back to Florida and begin my Psychotherapy practice again, I have to put things in perspective. There are going to be people talking about their adolescent acting out, their cosmetic surgery disappointments or some other comparatively mundane problem that really doesn't seem to matter much anymore. I have to keep my own personal feelings detached from my therapy clients. I cannot expect them to feel and relate to everything that I am feeling or relating to.*

I couldn't remove the verbal recollections of the "jumpers." It was as if I had flashed back to 1971, when I recalled a soldier returning from Viet Nam, hoping to receive some type of support and compassion from what he had gone through in the rice paddies as his buddies died in combat, ambushed around him. His story needed to be told back then. At least he and his oftentimes, too often ignored brave fellow Marines, as well as all the other armed service fighters for freedom, some who came back and some who did not, have a wall in Washington D.C. as a tribute to their bravery. New York City, as I write this and continue writing this book five years after 9/11, is still waiting for the beginning of construction of the building that will commemorate the brave souls who perished on that September morning that will take a prominent place in our country's history, and possibly legacy, for eternity. When I offered to speak at various public schools in South Florida about my 9/11 journey and not one principal even returned a phone call regarding my offer to share history with their students, I questioned my own take on reality. I began with an almost certain predictability from the intensity of the five days of CISD work in New York, to manifest my own symptoms of PTSD (Post Traumatic Stress Disorder). I felt alienated, alone, and I started drinking (a pastime I gave up after my college party days) and going out with some buddies until early in the A.M. My wife became more and more angry. My children were acting out.

* Note: In retrospect, approaching the five year anniversary of 9/11, as I re-write and interject

additional memories and descriptions of my perspective of 9/11, I recall that it was not my clients, but business and educational peers in the South Florida community who I expected more of an interest from to my experience in New York. There was somewhat of a dull, flat affective level of non-interest in both my recalling what I had just witnessed and professionally consulted, as well as incredulous though it may seem, an indignation and noticeable denial of wanting to address that the event even occurred. I remember feeling like a stranger in a strange land when I reentered the South Florida community upon returning from those days right after 9/11. I wanted to tell people about the tragic loss of life and how vulnerable we humans, we Americans are. Yes, there were the ritualistic, socialized events and commemorations with local political leaders, feigning empathy and caring to the victims and a pledge that they will, if elected, do everything they can to foster safety, freedom, and lower gas prices.

I was self-medicating and my life, both personally and professionally was in a tailspin. I was out of control. I was able to pull in the reins on my reactive behavior with the help of friends, family and my spouse. The period actually enabled me to put my priorities in order more than ever before. I began to take life more seriously and value and cherish each moment. I will not look back on my 9/11 experience and not feel sadness, but I will always feel proud that I contributed whatever I could for those five days in September 2001 and became a better person because of it.

I've been here. I've seen Ground Zero. I've seen the pain. I've heard the pain, and it is major pain. I am hoping that my proposal works. That the regional directors of this North American Express Division, agree with me that there should be a therapist on staff, at least for the next 6 months, someone who can be there everyday for the various people who are going to be in crisis. I am also recommending that I come back within two months to do follow up training with the staff for at least two or three days to pick up where we left off. I made some very good connections that day, contrary to the ludicrous situation that took place at the Executive Search Company on Wall Street. I guess I have to be tolerant of their attitude. It was their first week back at work and I suspect denial and shock were very much part of their emotional repertoire. Though I still find it ludicrous that someone actually made a complaint to the Atlanta Company that assigned me here, that I was too "direct" and "aggressive" in my approach to discussing the mission and format of critical incident work with the their staff during the pretraining meetings that I had with a couple of the top directors at Corporate Placement Inc.

I'll never forget the remark the coach of this company made as I spoke about my paradigm of PTSD debriefing, and what I expected to do with their company during the day when he told me that "we are a sophisticated group here." Sophisticated, non-sophisticated, again there are no lines of differential here. These people will feel and respond just like anyone else, eventually. The North American Express people were very responsive to my interventions and I hope to see them again. They all made it very clear to me that they were thankful that I was there, including Don, the manager.

Chapter X

Day 6

September 21, 2001

As I sat in the waiting area of the JFK airport, waiting for my return flight to Fort Lauderdale, I had a feeling of sadness from what I had seen and experienced that past week. I'm not sure whether I am ever going to be looking at therapeutic, as well as life issues, quite the same ever again. I'm not even sure of how the short or long term effects or impact on my own emotional well being will manifest from what I've seen and experienced in this past week (the subsequent impact is reflected on in the last chapter). All I know is that the terminal, which was typically much filled with people, was empty, with the exception of a few passengers waiting for departing flights. The scene in New York was still quite surrealistic, and I don't think that the reality of the attack had even come close to having the multitude of influences and effects that are still yet to occur.

It was just so strange to sit there on a normally, what I'm sure was a very busy Friday morning for flight travel. It looks like a morgue, for lack of a better terminology, an ironic choice of words on my part. People are certainly leery of flying in the New York area. I must admit, I had some thoughts of trepidation, but I have a belief in my position in life and faith and therefore flying does not present any more of a scare for me than does the potentiality of some other type of attack that these terrorists may make on this country at any place or at any time.

As my plane makes its final descent into the Fort Lauderdale airport, I reflect on how this was the saddest flight that I had ever taken. As I was reading accounts of the attack in the New York Times, the monumental strain and stress of what I have experienced in the past few days as a trauma-debriefing therapist all at once hit me. I began to cry, no weep, trying to contain it so it would not affect other passengers. I'll be home soon to my wife and two sons, to their questions and personal reactions. Soon after that, I'll be sitting in one of my two therapy locations, resuming my traditional therapy practice, but again knowing that that will never quite feel the same ever again.

Final Reflection

September 21, 2001

This is an anecdotal summary of the account that you have just read of the past several days of the debriefing counseling that I have done in the New York City area. As I think I mentioned in one of my reflections during this task, there was one gentleman out on Long Island who reflected on the experience of "seeing everyone being the color gray after the attack." He said, "everyone was gray, denomination, ethnic background, heritage, didn't matter, everyone was gray." I want to utilize this symbol, as well as that of the constant cloud that was still hovering above where the Twin Towers once stood, even upon my departure from New York City today.

First of all, as far as everyone being gray from the ash following the blasts and the subsequent second attack from the second jet and the collapse of the building, possibly this is an important message. Perhaps we need to listen and take heed to this message very strongly. As our warplanes prepare for obvious air strikes and our soldiers prepare for a land assault, it's not that I don't agree that we shouldn't retaliate; I firmly feel we have to do something. But on the other hand, war begets war: conflict begets conflict. I'm not sure what the answer is, but briefly for those moments or hours after the attacks everyone was the same color. Ironically that is what we should strive for, to discolor people and therefore not discount people because of their heritage or background, to rally around each other, to celebrate each other's different cultures and learn from them to enhance our own experience on Earth. As one woman put it during one of the debriefing preparatory sessions that I ran during the past week, she said, "We are all going to die anyway eventually, the terrorists, you and I; we are all going to die. Why should anyone want to speed up the process and cause such mutilation, disaster and pain?" I certainly couldn't answer that existential question, nor could I answer a lot of the questions that were forwarded to me during the week, though some of these questions were rhetorical in nature. I don't believe the person asking the question really wanted me to respond. But I do feel that the concrete reason for everyone being gray certainly was a very negative one. We should just try to bridge the ethnic, heritage, and religious gaps and not look negatively at the differences, but celebrate the differences to enhance our very short life on Earth as it is. Maybe this tragedy, this disaster, won't go for naught.

And as far as the cloud, unless you've been down at the Twin Towers, Wall Street area, it's hard to imagine how surrealistic this cloud is. After almost two weeks since the attacks, it is still there. I'm not sure whether it's smoke from the intense fire that once raged, or whether it's the dust and the ash of those deceased that still blows with the wind, or a combination of the two. But it's not lifting as of yet. I suspect as they continue to dig for remains and clear the area that could take weeks, months, I'm sure that that cloud will not dissipate and lift anytime soon and probably for good reasons. It's a reminder. It's a reminder that there is a cloud over all of us right now, a very dark cloud, a very painful cloud. My life has been altered significantly; my thoughts about life and everything included in that very broad area. That cloud remains. It remains as a reminder that if we truly want to see that cloud disappear, we have to not struggle, or kill, but join hands to rejoice in each others disparity, each other's differences, and let each one live the best type of life they can until the natural reaper of death grabs us all. That comes soon enough, often times with pain and sorrow, why hasten the process? Let the cloud lift, and let it lift with our love, our caring, and our work and compassion with one another. As the poignant lyric of a "Kansas" song summarizes our one common thread that ties all of us together as we end life, "all we are is dust in the wind."

Several Months Later

It has been several months since my critical incident counseling in the New York area. My life, as others lives, has gone on with a certain degree of predictability. Besides my clinical caseload, I continue to provide counseling for individuals who suffered unique and extraordinary trauma. I have most recently been working with victims from a violent bank robbery. Now, whenever I listen to people recounting of the incidents which have caused their trauma, I listen with a bit more sensitivity and compassion. Not that I didn't before, but the pain and anguish which still engulfs the lives of so many of the victims of 9/11 has made a special place in my psyche, an awareness that was not there before. I will at times, think of one of the many wonderful people who I encountered during those five life changing days in the New York metropolitan area. I wonder how they are doing. "Ground Zero" is being cleared and the cloud has lifted, but the psychological remnants and images are just as fresh as that nightmarish Tuesday on September 11, 2001. (Since the writing of this book, the entire Ground Zero has been cleared and a special ceremony was held to honor the dead.) Whenever I distract into a neurotic worry or self-indulgent behavior, I'm brought back to an important reality: We have each other. Each other's love, caring, friendship, and laughter. This is our main gift—each other. I cannot begin to understand the motivation of the pilots of the planes to plow into the Twin Towers. They just must have been miserable, depressed souls, beyond any religious, zealot orientation. Part of me remains in New York, possibly part of me merged with the surrealistic cloud that hovered just long enough to let us never forget, and always try with our best effort, to welcome all with love and caring.

Anecdote

Two Years Later (2003)

As I sit and watch the HBO Special on 9/11 this particular Sunday night, long after I have been back in the South Florida area, running and administering therapy and consulting in my clinical practice, I am brought back to the emotions I felt when I counseled individuals during those five special days in September of 2001. First and foremost, the great sadness. The pain comes roaring back as I watched the footage of the first, then the second plane, hitting the Twin Towers. Then the footage of the "jumpers," both videos and stills. It, again, was almost too surreal to believe. They looked like dolls, but they were all too human. Only seconds before their imminent death. I recalled the people I counseled in New York and the New York area during those emotional days. Their eyes were all the same. We call it "blunted" or "flat affect" in the field of Psychology. Eyes that were somewhere else, in another world, as I counseled them. Eyes of people who had seen "the jumpers," heard the "pop-pop" when the bodies hit the pavement. This was why their eyes were "flat." They had seen things on 9/11 that no one should ever have to see, especially innocent children who are not in a combat zone. That is why they "looked" at me when we spoke, that they were far away, not wanting to be in the world that was post 9/11 New York. Just like each night after I did five to eight hours of CISD counseling when I would feel emotions that I could not always identify, I had the same experience tonight. The sadness, horror, grief, anger, rage, vengefulness, inspired, and motivated. I could go on and on. One thing is for sure, it made me realize that what I did in the New York area during those five days in September 2001 was indeed one of the most profound and important professional experiences I could ever imagine to have. I'm glad that I could contribute my professional skills and caring for the individuals who physically survived, but who will have emotional scars for years to come. When I received a thank you letter from a Chief Executive from one of the client companies for whom I administered services to when in New York, I felt proud. When the tough New York manager, who now had to drive five hours to and from work every day, due to carpooling and relocation of his office to across the Hudson, took my hand and asked me to please speak with his upper management, I felt both good and concerned. This individual was seeing what was to come. He was seeing that the long drives, the anguish, fear, stress, terror, nightmares and lost sleep, would gather up in him and staff. So watching the HBO Special tonight brought his image back to me and I cried. The letter from the executive was nice*, but I wonder whether the surviving "victims" are receiving the psychological help, which is so very important for months, even for years to come. Only time will tell.

* Though this company did not feel it was necessary to follow-through with the intensive interventions, which I also recommended after my days with his employees.

www.ingramcontent.com/pod-product-compliance
Lightning Source LLC
Chambersburg PA
CBHW031304280526
45784CB00004B/1988